Artists in Their Time

Paul Gauguin

Robert Anderson

Franklin Watts
A Division of Scholastic Inc.
New York Toronto London Auckland Sydney
Mexico City New Delhi Hong Kong
Danbury, Connecticut

First published in 2003 by
Franklin Watts
96 Leonard Street
London EC2A 4XD

First American edition published
in 2003 by Franklin Watts
A Division of Scholastic Inc.
90 Sherman Turnpike
Danbury, CT 06816

Series Editor: Adrian Cole
Editor: Jill A. Laidlaw
Series Designer: Mo Choy
Art Director: Jonathan Hair
Picture Researcher: Kathy Lockley

A CIP catalog record for this title
is available from the Library of Congress.

ISBN 0-531-12239-5 (Lib. Bdg.)
ISBN 0-531-16647-3 (Pbk.)

Printed in Hong Kong, China

Acknowledgements

Jules Agostini: 36B. AKG London 10 B, 20 T, 26, 32 B + Cover BC. Art Institute of Chicago, Il. Bridgeman
Art Library, London: 12B. Bibliotheque Nationale, Paris: AKG London: 20 B. Museu Calouste Gulbenkian,
Lisbon: Bridgeman Art Library, London: 15T. © CAP-Viollet: 14B. Danske Kunstindustrimuseet, Copenhagen.
Photo: Pernille Klemp: 24BL. Mary Evans Picture Library/Explorer Archives: 41B. Israel Museum, Jerusalem.
Photo: Erich Lessing/AKG London: 33 B. Sylvain Grandadam/Robert Harding Picture Library: 38B. Haags
Gemeentemuseum, Netherlands: Bridgeman Art Library, London: 27B. Robert Harding Picture Library: 14T,
18T, 28T. © Harlingue-Viollet: 8B, 15B, 16T, Hotel de Ville, Paris: Bridgeman Art Library, London: 27T.
Kimbell Art Museum, Fort Worth, Texas. Photo: Erich Lessing/AKG London: 11, © LL-Viollet: 24CR. Musée
du Louvre, Paris. Photo: RMN-Michele Bellot: 18B ©ADAGP, Paris & DACS, London 2003; Photo: Gerard
Blot: 38T. © Lee Miller Archives: 40B. Mairie de Montreuil. Photo: Erich Lessing/AKG London: 36T.©
ADAGP, Paris & DACS, London 2003. Musée Departemental Maurice Denis le Prieuré, St-Germain-en-Laye,
France: 6T. Museum of Fine Arts, Boston, Mass.:Bridgeman Art Library, London: 37. National Gallery of
Scotland, Edinburgh: Bridgeman Art Library, London: 17, 19. Neue Pinakothek, Munich: AKG London 22 B;
Bridgeman Art Library, London: 13. Ny Carlsberg Glyptotek, Copenhagen. Photo: Erich Lessing/AKG London:
9 T; Bridgeman Art Library, London: 31. Oeffentliche Kunstsammlung, Basel: AKG London: 39. Musee d'Orsay,
Paris: Bridgeman Art Library, London: 24TL, 25, 30B, 35, Cover C. Geoff Renner/Robert Harding Picture
Library: 34B, Cover BR. Carlos Reyes-Manzo/Andes Press Agency: 7. Musée Royaux des Beaux-Arts de
Belgique, Brussels: Bridgeman Art Library, London: 29. Stadtische Galerie im Lenbachhaus, Munich:
Bridgeman Art Library, London: 40T. Stockholm National Museum: AKG London: 9 B. United
Artists/Courtesy Kobal Collection: 41T. Van Gogh Museum, Amsterdam: 23; Artothek: 42; Bridgeman Art
Library, London: 21. Victoria & Albert Museum, London: Bridgeman Art Library, London: 34 T. © Collection
Viollet: 8, 16B, 22T, 28B, Cover BL. Whitford & Hughes, London: Bridgeman Art Library, London: 33 T.

Whilst every attempt has been made to clear copyright
should there be any inadvertent omission please apply
in the first instance to the publisher regarding rectification

Contents

Who Was Paul Gauguin?   6

Back to France   8

Poverty and Exile   10

Searching for a Style   12

Brittany   14

A Caribbean Island   16

Synthetism   18

Theo and Vincent   20

Trouble in the South   22

The Universal Exhibition   24

Symbolism   26

Le Pouldu   28

Escape to the Tropics   30

Tahiti   32

In Search of Recognition   34

Depression and Despair   36

Final Days   38

Gauguin's Legacy   40

Friends and Foes   42

Timeline   42

Glossary   44

Museums and Galleries   45

Index   46

Who Was Paul Gauguin?

Paul Gauguin was one of the great pioneers of modern art. Searching for inspiration, he lived and worked in wild and distant places – from the windswept peninsula of Brittany in France to the tropical island of Tahiti. Gauguin's masterpieces radiate color and energy. They have inspired generations of artists to work freely, imaginatively, and courageously.

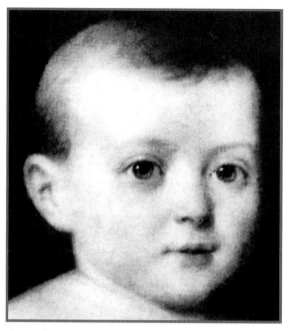

▲ *Paul Gauguin at the Age of Two*, c.1850, Jules Laure.

▼ Flora Tristan (1803-44), Gauguin's grandmother, was a successful author who wrote *Wanderings of an Outcast* (1838), a book about her trip around Peru in 1833-34. She also wrote books about France and England. Gauguin kept copies of her work with him all of his life.

THE SECOND EMPIRE

Paul Gauguin was born on June 7, 1848, in Paris, France. His father, Clovis Gauguin (1814-51), was a journalist. His mother, Aline (1826-67), was related to a rich and wealthy family of Spanish aristocrats who had moved to Peru during the 17th century.

In the year of Gauguin's birth, revolutionaries in France overthrew the king and made the country a republic. However, the Republic lasted less than a year. Prince Louis-Napoléon (1808-73), the nephew of Napoléon Bonaparte, was elected President of France in 1850 but later declared himself Emperor (December 1851) with the title of Napoleon III. The period of Napoleon III's rule (1851-70) is known as the Second Empire.

TIMELINE ▶

June 7, 1848	February 1850	October 1851	December 2, 1851
Paul Gauguin is born in Paris.	Prince Louis-Napoléon Bonaparte is elected president of France.	Gauguin's family leaves for Peru; his father dies on the way.	Louis-Napoléon Bonaparte becomes Emperor of France.

ESCAPE TO PERU

Gauguin's father disliked Louis-Napoléon and supported the revolution. Disappointed with his country, he decided to go to Peru to set up a newspaper. In October of 1851, he and his wife set sail from France with their two young children, Marie (age four) and Paul (age three).

The voyage to Peru was long and dangerous. As the Gauguins' ship rounded the southern tip of South America, Clovis Gauguin died very suddenly. Gauguin's mother had no choice but to continue the journey to Lima, the capital of Peru, with her children. There, Aline's great-uncle, Don Pio de Tristan Moscoso (1769-1856), welcomed the family into his home.

The Gauguin family lived in comfort and luxury for four years. Lima was a lively and beautiful city and always seemed to be bathed in brilliant sunshine. The city's houses were painted in bright colors, and its people were famous for their extravagant clothes and their hospitality. To the east of Lima soared the snowcapped mountains of the Andes. To the west stretched the clear blue waters of the Pacific Ocean. There were lush tropical plants and trees, and exotic animals and birds everywhere. For the young Gauguin, it seemed like paradise.

▲ The Peruvian capital, Lima, has many beautiful buildings and wide, busy streets. This is the Plaza de Armas, a popular place to walk, meet, or sit.

Back to France

In 1854, political unrest in Peru forced the Gauguin family to return to France where they settled in Saint-Marceau, an area of Orléans where Gauguin's paternal grandparents lived. When Gauguin was 11 he was sent to boarding school just outside of Orléans, and his mother moved to Paris and opened a dressmaking shop. Gauguin's teachers thought he was an odd and difficult student. Gauguin was very unhappy. He dreamed of escaping France and returning to the sunshine and heat of the Tropics.

▲ Crew on a merchant navy sailing ship in the 1870s. Gauguin would have done work similar to the deckhands in this photograph.

A SEAMAN

In 1865, at age 17, Gauguin went to sea as an apprentice. Over the next five years, Gauguin crisscrossed the Atlantic and Pacific Oceans and visited countries all over the world. He also took part in the Franco-Prussian War (July 1870-May 1871). In 1871, Gauguin left the navy and returned to Paris. The war had brought an end to the Second Empire, and France was a republic once more.

A MARRIED MAN

Gauguin's mother died in 1867. A friend of hers, Gustave Arosa – a rich businessman and amateur photographer – found Gauguin a job as a stockbroker on the Paris stock exchange. Gauguin was immediately successful. In 1873, he met and fell in love with a young Danish woman named Mette Gad (1850-1920). The couple married in 1873 and settled in a comfortable home in a Paris suburb. They had five children – four sons (Emil, Clovis, Jean-René, and Paul Rollon) and one daughter (Aline).

▲ Gauguin around the time when he became a stockbroker in Paris.

TIMELINE ▶

1854	1865	1867	1870–71	April 1871	November 22, 1873	1882	1883
Gauguin's family returns to France.	Gauguin joins the merchant navy.	Gauguin's mother dies.	The Franco-Prussian War. The start of the Third Republic.	Gauguin returns to Paris and becomes a stockbroker.	Gauguin marries Mette Gad; he becomes a "Sunday painter."	The French stock market collapses.	After losing his job, Gauguin becomes a full-time painter.

A SUNDAY PAINTER

Gauguin was interested in art, especially Impressionist art (see panel). He began to collect paintings but wasn't happy just buying pictures, he wanted to create them, too. With his friend Emile Schuffenecker (1851-1934), a fellow stockbroker, he went to evening classes at an art school in Paris. For most of the week he worked hard at the office and only found time to paint on Sundays. At first he painted in a very traditional way, but gradually became more and more influenced by the Impressionist style. In 1879, the Impressionist painter Camille Pissarro (1830-1903) invited Gauguin to show his paintings at the fourth Impressionist exhibition – a great honor for a "Sunday painter."

▲ *The Garden in the Rue Carcel*, **1881.** Early in his career, Gauguin painted in an Impressionist style (above). This picture shows Gauguin's wife, Mette, and three of their children relaxing in their pretty garden. It is one of the artist's happiest paintings and is full of his tender feelings for his family.

Perhaps Gauguin would have remained just a talented amateur artist had it not been for the collapse of the French stock exchange in January of 1882. By September of 1883, at the age of 34, Gauguin had lost his job, and instead of finding a new one he decided to paint full-time. He proudly declared: "From now on I will paint every day."

THE IMPRESSIONISTS

The Impressionist movement began in the 1870s, and the first Impressionist exhibition was held in 1874. The Impressionists painted brilliantly colored pictures of the streets and cafés of Paris and of the French countryside. In their pictures, they tried to capture the passing effects of light and weather. For example, they painted snow not just as pure white but as an array of glistening blues and greens and frosty pinks. The Impressionists were among the first artists to paint outdoors in front of their subject, instead of in a studio. Claude Monet (1840-1926), one of the leading Impressionist artists, was famous for painting outside even on the coldest days.

◀ *Peasant Pushing a Wheelbarrow*, **1874, Camille Pissarro.** Gauguin's friend and teacher, Camille Pissarro, painted this picture near his country home in Pontoise. The painting's bright, sunny colors and broad, free brushstrokes are typical of many Impressionist works.

Poverty and Exile

▲ Mette and her five children, in a photograph taken in 1888.

GAUGUIN'S FAMILY

Gauguin and his wife did not live together again after 1885, but they wrote to each other – Gauguin with news of his experiences as a painter, and Mette with news of the children. Money was always a source of tension as Mette struggled to support five children by working as a teacher. Gauguin rarely sent money – in fact Mette often sent him money! Despite Mette's support of the children, Gauguin often criticized his wife publicly – perhaps, deep down, he was ashamed of his treatment of his family and wished to turn attention away from his abandonment of them.

Without a steady job Gauguin had to give up his comfortable house in Paris. He took his family to live in Rouen – a city to the west of the capital – where he hoped they could live more cheaply. Gauguin worked very hard but was not able to sell a single painting. In desperation, his wife, Mette, decided to take the children to live with her parents in Copenhagen, Denmark.

COPENHAGEN

Gauguin continued to struggle with his work, but he soon followed his family to Denmark. Mette's family disapproved of Gauguin because they thought he was selfish to sacrifice the comfort of his wife and children to pursue his dream of becoming an artist. Gauguin felt lonely and isolated. At the same time, however, he grew more sure of his talent as an artist. In *Self-Portrait* (opposite), painted in Mette's parents' home, he shows himself hard at work: he was determined to become a painter whatever the consequences.

◄ This is a view of Copenhagen, Denmark, around 1885, when Mette and the children moved there. In the 19th century Copenhagen was one of Europe's busiest ports.

PARIS

By the summer of 1885, Gauguin could no longer bear to stay in Copenhagen. He returned to Paris taking his second-oldest son, the six-year-old Clovis, with him but leaving the rest of his family behind.

TIMELINE ▶

January 1884	July 1884	November 1884	June 1885
Gauguin takes his family to live in Rouen.	Mette Gauguin takes the children to live in Copenhagen, Denmark. Gauguin stays in Rouen.	Gauguin joins his family in Copenhagen.	Gauguin returns to Paris with his six-year-old son, Clovis.

Self-Portrait, 1885
oil on canvas, 25 1/2 x 21 3/8 in (65 x 54.3 cm), Kimball Art Museum, Fort Worth, Texas

In the painting we can see Gauguin's canvas, his brush, and his artist's palette, smeared with oil paint. Because he is painting his mirror image, Gauguin shows himself painting with his left hand. In fact he was right-handed! The dark, heavy colors of this self-portrait are very different to the bright colors that Gauguin used in his later work.

Searching for a Style

ARTISTS GO DOTTY!

In the early 1880s, some young artists wanted to create a new kind of art that was more serious than the "snapshots" painted by the Impressionists. Georges Seurat and Paul Signac (1863-1935) developed a new way of painting using tiny dots of pure color placed next to each other. When seen from a distance, the dots appear to fuse, creating a new, different color. This art movement is usually called Pointillism, from the French word for "dot" – point.

In Paris, Gauguin and Clovis lived in a cold, miserable apartment. Gauguin earned money doing odd jobs, such as sticking posters up in the street, and was so busy trying to make ends meet that he hardly found time to paint. Clovis got sick and Gauguin's sister, Marie, had to take care of him. Although Gauguin missed his children very much, his determination to be an artist took first place.

SEARCHING FOR INSPIRATION

In early 1886, Gauguin showed some of his paintings at the eighth Impressionist exhibition. Art critics hardly noticed his work at all. Instead, the star of the show was a brilliant young artist named Georges Seurat (1859-91, see panel).

Gauguin was restless and unhappy; he felt that, unlike Seurat, he had not yet found his own way of painting. In the summer of 1886, Gauguin left Clovis in Paris with his sister and went to Brittany, a remote region of France bordering the Atlantic Ocean. There, he hoped, he would be able to find the inspiration he needed to create his own artistic style. It was in Brittany that he painted *Four Breton Women*.

◀ *Sunday Afternoon on the Island of La Grande Jatte,* 1884-86, Georges Seurat. This whole picture is painted with thousands of tiny dots of unmixed color.

TIMELINE ▶

Spring 1886	May 1886
Pointillist painter Georges Seurat completes *Sunday Afternoon on the Island of La Grande Jatte*.	Gauguin shows his work at the eighth Impressionist exhibition.

Four Breton Women, 1886

oil on canvas, 28 ^{1}/$_3$ x 35 ^{2}/$_5$ in (72 x 90 cm), Neue Pinakothek, Munich, Germany

Four Breton Women features women wearing the traditional Breton costume of a white headdress, shawl, and clogs. This picture shows a change in Gauguin's painting technique – instead of blending colors together as the Impressionists did, Gauguin has started to outline large areas of color, such as the women's headdresses and collars. This makes the women's headdresses and collars look like a decorative pattern dancing across the top half of the picture.

"I have finally found the money for my trip to Brittany...
My painting arouses a lot of discussion and I must say
that Americans rather like it."

Paul Gauguin

Brittany

Brittany is a large peninsula in the far west of France. It is famous for its rocky coastline, bleak moors, and ancient stone circles; for many people its name conjures up an aura of mystery and magic. Brittany's inhabitants – the Bretons – are a Celtic people closely related to the Welsh, Scottish, Irish, and Cornish peoples of Britain. They first came to the region in the 5th and 6th centuries A.D.

▲ Brittany lies in the far west of France, and its coastline is rugged and beautiful. To the north, across the English Channel, is another Celtic region – Cornwall.

A UNIQUE CULTURE

Until late in the 15th century, Brittany was an independent country, separate from France. Even after the region became part of France, the Bretons remained fiercely proud of their culture and traditions. Today, many Bretons still speak the ancient Breton language, and some believe that Brittany should be separate from France.

Over the centuries the Bretons developed a culture that was very different from that of the rest of France. For example, they had their own music, featuring a special kind of bagpipe known as a *biniou*. They had their own local food and drink, including the delicious buckwheat pancakes known as *crêpes* and a kind of honey wine, or mead, called *clouchen*. Even Breton beds were different. Traditionally, Breton people slept inside a wooden, box-like bunk, called a *lit-clos*, or "closed bed."

▲ This pardon, or religious festival, (shown above in the 1880s) takes place in Brittany every year on September 8.

TIMELINE ▶

July 1886	October 1886	Winter 1886
Gauguin goes to Pont-Aven in Brittany.	Gauguin returns to Paris.	Gauguin works on *Four Breton Women* in Paris.

▲ *Breton Women at a Pardon*, 1887, Pascal-Adolphe-Jean Dagnan-Bouveret (1852-1929). This painting shows Breton men and women dressed in their traditional clothes at a pardon.

"I find wildness and primitiveness there. When my wooden shoes ring out on its granite soil, I hear the muffled, dull, and powerful note I am looking for in my painting."

Paul Gauguin

RELIGIOUS PEOPLE

The Bretons were very religious. They set up imposing stone shrines called calvaries near churches and at crossroads. The calvaries were usually just simple crosses. Sometimes, however, they were elaborate sculptures showing Christ on the cross surrounded by his mourning disciples. The Bretons also held religious festivals called *pardons*. During a pardon, pilgrims came from miles around to hear solemn sermons and take part in religious processions.

TOURISTS

Until the 19th century, people in other parts of France thought of Brittany as a remote and primitive region. During the 19th century, more and more tourists began to visit Brittany using the newly built railroad. By this time, many Breton customs were already dying out. For example, Breton women now only wore their traditional costumes on Sundays or at pardons.

PONT-AVEN

Brittany attracted artists as well as tourists. One of the most popular places for artists to live was Pont-Aven – and it was here that Gauguin made several long stays. Many European artists were leaving big, industrial cities during this period in order to live and paint in the countryside. They hoped that by living close to nature they could make their art more powerful and direct. Gauguin also believed that Brittany was a wild and beautiful place, rich in history and myth, that could inspire him to create a new way of painting (see *Four Breton Women* on page 13).

▲ This is the boarding house that Gauguin lived in at Pont-Aven. Gauguin is in the first row, seated second from the left.

A Caribbean Island

▲ Construction work on the Panama Canal, c. 1890.

THE PANAMA CANAL

Despite the fact that Gauguin's sister Marie was living in Panama City with her husband, Gauguin and Laval found Panama an unfriendly place and planned to leave it as soon as possible. They got jobs as temporary clerks with a French company that was about to start building the huge Panama Canal, linking the Atlantic and Pacific Oceans. After two weeks, the two artists had enough money to travel to Martinique. However, it would be much longer before work on the canal was complete. The French started to build it in 1879, but gave up in 1898 because of the high costs. The 40-mile (64-km) long canal was finally opened to ships in 1914.

Throughout his life Gauguin dreamt of the happiness and security he had known as a child in Peru. He was always making plans to escape his difficult and poor life in France to find freedom and ease in a distant paradise. The first "paradise" Gauguin discovered was Brittany; next he chose Panama in Central America. Gauguin wrote to Mette and asked her to come and get Clovis so that he could go traveling. On April 10, 1887, Gauguin left France for Panama, accompanied by Charles Laval (1861-94), a painter he had met in Pont-Aven.

MARTINIQUE

Gauguin's stay in Panama was brief (see panel). His new paradise turned out to be Martinique, a beautiful Caribbean island that he and Laval had glimpsed on their way to Panama. Gauguin was inspired by the island's sunlight and jewel-like colors to paint some of his boldest pictures yet, including *Tropical Vegetation* (opposite).

Gauguin stayed in Martinique for only four months. He and Laval became very ill with malaria. Once his friend Schuffenecker sent him his fare home, Gauguin left for Paris.

▲ As well as tropical forests and small villages, Martinique also had elegant colonial architecture, built by the French authorities.

TIMELINE ▶

April 10, 1887	April 30, 1887	June 1887	November 1887
Gauguin sails for Panama with the painter Charles Laval.	Gauguin and Laval arrive in Panama.	Gauguin and Laval travel to Martinique.	Gauguin returns to Paris, leaving Laval (who is still ill) in Martinique.

Tropical Vegetation, 1887

oil on canvas, 45 2/3 x 35 in (116 x 89 cm), National Gallery of Scotland, Edinburgh, Scotland

The tropical island of Martinique must have reminded Gauguin of Peru. In this painting, the lush, glowing landscape looks almost like a vision of paradise. Only the deep-blue sea and pale, sunlit sky give us a sense of looking into the distance – everything else is vegetation.

Synthetism

▲ Synthetist artists took inspiration from stained glass windows (above) to include areas of flat color outlined with black in their pictures.

THE SCHOOL OF PONT-AVEN

By the late 1880s and early 1890s, the Synthetist style developed by Gauguin and Bernard was being imitated by many young artists, including Jacob Meyer de Hann (1851-95) and Maurice Denis (1870-1943). Many of them flocked to Pont-Aven, where they painted the local people, the countryside, and religious rituals. Some of these painters used the new style to express their Christian beliefs, setting biblical stories in the Breton landscape just as Gauguin had done in *The Vision After the Sermon*. Soon people were speaking of a new style, or "school," of painting – the School of Pont-Aven.

After a few months back in Paris, Gauguin left for Pont-Aven, where his meeting with an ambitious young artist named Émile Bernard (1868-1941) was to transform the way he painted.

PAINTING FROM MEMORY

Bernard's pictures were even more daring than Gauguin's. They featured areas of bright, flat color surrounded by thick, black lines. Bernard and Gauguin decided that it was important to paint pictures from memory or imagination rather than from real life, and that these scenes should be full of simplified colors and forms. Bernard and Gauguin hoped to convey strong emotions that would reveal the "truth" of the subject in their pictures. This new style of painting was called Synthetism or Cloisonnism.

◀ In this sketch, Émile Bernard depicted himself (center), Gauguin (right), and Schuffenecker (left) as the leaders of the new style of painting called Synthetism.

JACOB AND THE ANGEL

The Vision After the Sermon (opposite) is one of the first pictures painted by Gauguin in the Synthetist style. The picture shows a group of Breton women experiencing a vision of Jacob wrestling with an angel – an episode from the Bible (Genesis 32: 24-30). Once Jacob had wrestled with the angel he received his blessing.

TIMELINE ▶

November 1887	February 1888	Summer 1888	August–September 1888
Gauguin arrives back in Paris from Martinique.	Gauguin leaves Paris for Pont-Aven.	Gauguin meets the painter Émile Bernard.	Gauguin paints *The Vision After the Sermon*.

The Vision After the Sermon, 1888

oil on canvas, 28 3/4 x 36 1/4 in (73 x 92 cm), National Gallery of Scotland, Edinburgh, Scotland

The women in the picture can "see" Jacob wrestling with the angel, even though all but one of them has their eyes closed, because they are in a religious trance. This picture is highly symbolic (see pages 26-27) – Gauguin shows both the Breton women and Jacob and the angel in the same place, separated only by a tree trunk. For the very religious Breton women, Gauguin seems to be saying that the world of the Bible is every bit as real, and as close, as the fields and trees. This picture is a move by Gauguin away from the simple "snapshots" of the world painted by the Impressionists (see page 9).

"A hint: don't paint too much after nature."

Paul Gauguin

Theo and Vincent

▲ The artist Vincent van Gogh, in a photograph taken in 1871.

VINCENT VAN GOGH

Vincent van Gogh, like Gauguin, was a Post-Impressionist artist. This means that he was greatly influenced by the Impressionists but took art one step further by creating a new style all his own – he would load up his brush with paint and slap it thickly onto the canvas in dynamic daubs of color. In doing so, he gave the pictures he painted an emotional intensity seldom seen in the Impressionists' work. This was partly a reflection of his own passionate and idealistic nature.

After his return from Martinique, Gauguin got to know two Dutch brothers living in Paris – Vincent (1853-90) and Theo (1857-91) van Gogh. The brothers admired Gauguin's work. Vincent was a brilliant but struggling painter. Theo was a successful art dealer who paid Gauguin a certain amount of money every month in exchange for pictures to sell in the gallery he managed.

AN INVITATION

The three friends wrote many letters to each other, exchanging their ideas about art. In 1888, Theo suggested that Gauguin join his brother Vincent in southern France. Theo believed that the two artists would work well together. Vincent dreamed of setting up a "Studio of the South" and he saw Gauguin as the first important artist to join him there. Gauguin, always short of money, was tempted by Theo's offer to pay his expenses as long as he lived with Vincent.

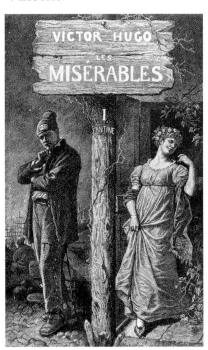

A GIFT

Before Gauguin joined Vincent, he sent him this striking self-portrait (opposite). The painting is very different from the gloomy self-portrait Gauguin painted several years earlier in Copenhagen (see page 11). Here Gauguin's green jacket contrasts with the flowery, yellow wallpaper behind, as the artist stares out at us like a sly fox.

◀ The title page of an 1879 edition of *Les Misérables* (see opposite).

TIMELINE ▶

1888	October 3, 1888
Theo van Gogh writes to Gauguin suggesting that he join his brother, Vincent, in southern France.	Vincent van Gogh writes to Gauguin about his plans for a "Studio of the South."

Self-Portrait: Les Misérables, 1888

oil on canvas, 17 $^5/_7$ x 21 $^3/_5$ in (45 x 55 cm), Van Gogh Museum, Vincent van Gogh Foundation, Amsterdam, The Netherlands

In the right-hand corner of this self-portrait, Gauguin wrote the words "Les Misérables: To my friend Vincent."
Les Misérables ("The Unhappy") is the title of a popular novel by Victor Hugo (1802-85), one of the greatest writers of 19th-century France. The hero of *Les Misérables* is Jean Valjean, a criminal who decides to begin a new and better life but is hounded by a vengeful police officer. By calling his picture *Les Misérables*, Gauguin was suggesting that both he and Émile Bernard, whose portrait hangs behind him, were persecuted because they were daring to be different.

In *Les Misérables* Gauguin began to develop some of the images that he used in his later work. Look at the background of *Les Misérables* – it is similar to the background of *Vahine no te Tiare* on page 31.

"I have done the self-portrait Vincent asked for. I believe it is one of my best things ... the color is far from nature; imagine ... pottery contorted by a great fire!"

Paul Gauguin

Trouble in the South

DIFFERENT WAYS OF PAINTING

Like the Impressionists, van Gogh painted exactly what he saw in front of him. He painted with vigorous, swirling brush-strokes that were charged with energy.

Gauguin painted from his imagination. He took inspiration from the things he saw – such as a landscape or a work of art – and recorded his impressions of these things in sketches. Then he used his memories and drawings to create pictures that were imaginary.

▲ The "Yellow House" in Arles, where van Gogh and Gauguin lived.

▲ *Vase With Twelve Sunflowers*, 1888, Vincent van Gogh. Van Gogh painted a series of sunflower pictures to celebrate Gauguin's arrival.

In October of 1888, Gauguin went to live with Vincent van Gogh in Arles, a town in the far south of France. Van Gogh was lonely so he was delighted that Gauguin had joined him. Gauguin was flattered by van Gogh's enthusiasm at seeing him and also wanted to please Theo van Gogh since he was promoting Gauguin's work in Paris. At first the two artists got along well. They worked hard and encouraged each other. They discussed their ideas and produced about 20 paintings each.

OPPOSITES

Gauguin and van Gogh worked in very different ways, and each became convinced that the other artist was painting in the wrong way. They started to fight and get on each others' nerves. Van Gogh was hurt by Gauguin's criticisms and crushed by his overbearing personality. On December 23, van Gogh and Gauguin had a violent argument. Gauguin left the studio he shared with van Gogh and fled to a boarding house. Van Gogh was so depressed that he cut off part of his left ear. Gauguin went back to Paris where he stayed with his friend Schuffenecker.

TIMELINE ▶

October 23, 1888	December 23, 1888	December 25, 1888	January 7, 1889
Gauguin joins Vincent van Gogh in Arles. They live in the Yellow House.	Gauguin and van Gogh have a violent argument. Gauguin leaves. Van Gogh becomes upset and cuts off part of his left ear. The next morning he is taken to the hospital.	Van Gogh is unconscious for two days.	Vincent van Gogh leaves the hospital and returns to the Yellow House alone.

Portrait of Vincent van Gogh Painting Sunflowers, 1888

oil on canvas, 28 3/4 x 35 4/5 in (73 x 91 cm), Van Gogh Museum, Vincent van Gogh Foundation, Amsterdam, The Netherlands

Can you spot something strange about the viewpoint in this picture? Gauguin paints van Gogh from above, so that we can see both the top of the table and van Gogh's palette at the same time. Gauguin also used very bold colors. For example, the rich orange sunflowers contrast with the blue vase. There are hardly any shadows, and the whole picture seems to burn with the bright light of southern France.

"Vincent and I don't agree on much, and especially not on painting."

Paul Gauguin

The Universal Exhibition

▲ *Be Mysterious*, **1889.** Gauguin was one of the first sculptors of his time to return to the medieval practice of painting wood carvings.

GAUGUIN THE SCULPTOR

As a young man, Gauguin had learned to sculpt as well as paint. He carved a beautiful, dreamy portrait of his wife out of marble. He continued to experiment with sculpture throughout his life. Just as his painting became simpler and bolder, so did his sculpture. In Brittany, he was inspired by the local traditional wood carving. In 1889 he experimented with pottery, making a mug in the shape of his own head (right). Later, in Polynesia, Gauguin devoted a lot of his time to sculpture, even carving the wooden posts and beams of the houses he lived in.

▶ Gauguin made this pottery mug in the shape of his own head.

In February of 1889, Gauguin returned to live in Pont-Aven. In May, however, he traveled to Paris to visit the Universal Exhibition, a grand exhibition that was held in celebration of the centennial of the French Revolution (1789). Millions of people came to the French capital to see exhibits from all over the world. Gauguin visited the exhibition many times. He was especially fascinated by the displays sent from the countries of the French Empire, including part of a Buddhist temple from Java, Indonesia, and a Moroccan bazaar (below).

◀ The Moroccan bazaar as it was at the Universal Exhibition of 1889. Bazaar is the Persian word for market.

THE CAFE VOLPINI

The Universal Exhibition also included a display of French art. The authorities thought that Gauguin's work was too new and shocking to include in the main exhibition. Instead, Gauguin and his artist friends such as Bernard, Laval, and Schuffenecker, showed their work at the Café Volpini in the exhibition grounds. Most people paid little attention to Gauguin's work, but a small band of artists and critics named Gauguin the leader of the Symbolist painters (see pages 26-27).

TIMELINE ▶

February 1889	May 6, 1889	Summer 1889
Gauguin returns to Brittany from Paris.	The Universal Exhibition begins in Paris and stays open for the next six months.	Gauguin and his friends hold an exhibition of their work at the Café Volpini.

The Schuffenecker Family, 1889

oil on canvas, 28 3/4 x 36 1/4 in (73 x 92 cm), Musée d'Orsay, Paris, France

One of the attractions at the Universal Exhibition was a display of Japanese art featuring artists such as Katsushika Hokusai (1760-1849) and Ando Hiroshige (1797-1858). Many Western artists, including Gauguin, were inspired by the Japanese painters' flat, shadowless colors and simple, bold designs. In *The Schuffenecker Family*, Gauguin used this inspiration to create a jigsaw of colorful shapes – he even included a Japanese print in the painting (in the background, far right).

"I am going through such a phase of disillusionment that I cannot help yelling out loud …"

Paul Gauguin

Symbolism

Throughout history, artists and writers all over the world have used symbols in their drawings, paintings, sculptures, and novels. A symbol is an image of an object or person that represents something invisible, such as an idea or a feeling.

Religious paintings often contain symbols. One symbol often found in Christian art is the halo – the circle of golden light shown around the head of a saint. The halo is not a real object but a symbol of the saint's holiness.

THE REALISTS

In the mid-19th century, a group of artists called the Realists decided to avoid using symbols in their paintings. Instead, they tried showing only the everyday world around them as honestly as they could.

The Impressionist painters developed the Realists' ideas further. They strove to capture even the most fleeting appearances of the visible world – for example, mist drifting over a river or a railroad station filled with billowing smoke.

THE SYMBOLISTS

During the 1880s, many young artists rebelled against the ideas of the Realists and Impressionists. This new art movement was called Symbolism.

The Symbolists believed that paintings showing only the outside appearance of things were unimportant. Instead, they wanted to paint pictures that would explore their feelings and thoughts and show spiritual and religious ideas. A painting, they believed, should reveal emotions and truths.

▲ Stéphane Mallarmé, the leading Symbolist poet.

STÉPHANE MALLARMÉ

The greatest Symbolist poet was Stéphane Mallarmé (1842-98). Mallarmé created his poems out of the sounds of words, just as a composer uses notes in music. Mallarmé believed it was possible to suggest emotions beyond the matter-of-fact meaning of the words in this way. Poems, Mallarmé declared, should be full of mystery. Most of the pleasure of reading them lay in trying to imagine what they could be about, he said. This idea greatly appealed to Gauguin. Like other artists, he recognized it could be applied to painting as well as poems. It was up to the people looking at his works to imagine what it meant.

◀ *Winter*, 1884-93, **Pierre Puvis de Chavannes.** This painting is one of a pair – Puvis de Chavannes also painted a picture called Summer. Each painting summed up the season it represented in a poetic way.

ARTISTS

The first Symbolists were writers and poets (see panel) but painters soon adopted Symbolist ideas. Some used symbols in their work in a straightforward way. For example, Pierre Puvis de Chavannes (1824-98) painted a mural, or wall painting, called *Winter* (above) which showed villagers trying to keep warm in a cold landscape of snow and leafless trees. The old man in the ruined building on the left is a symbol for the season since he is in the winter (at the end) of his life. Other artists used symbols that are much harder to understand. The drawings of Odilon Redon (1840-1916) are full of mystery and menace, and it is hard to understand what they mean.

GAUGUIN AND THE SYMBOLISTS

Gauguin became friendly with many Symbolist painters and writers, including Mallarmé and Redon, in the late 1880s. As a result, Gauguin came to use color and line like musical notes rather than to describe the ordinary appearance of an object. He once declared: "By arranging colors and lines … I achieve symphonies and harmonies that make people think just like music makes people think." Like Mallarmé's poems and Redon's drawings, Gauguin's paintings are strange and mysterious.

"[The Impressionists] heed only the eye and neglect the mysterious centers of thought."

Paul Gauguin

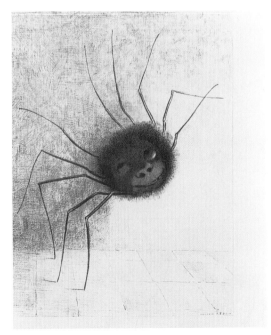

▲ *The Laughing Spider*, **1881, Odilon Redon.** Redon's charcoal drawings include huge, greedy-looking spiders and plants with human heads.

27

Le Pouldu

Gauguin returned to Pont-Aven in October of 1889, but thought that it had become overcrowded with tourists and went to live at a nearby hamlet called Le Pouldu. With him were Paul Sérusier (1863-1927) (see page 30) and the Dutch painter Jacob Meyer de Haan (see page 18).

A HARD LIFE

Apart from a few scattered farms, there was not much at Le Pouldu except bare sand dunes and craggy rocks. The weather was often cold, rainy, and windy, and life for the local people was very hard. The harshness of Le Pouldu inspired some of Gauguin's boldest paintings. In *The Green Christ* (opposite), a woman rests beside a calvary that shows Christ being taken down from the cross. Behind her are the steely-blue sea and the sand dunes of Le Pouldu.

▲ The Sacré-Coeur in Paris was built as a result of the French revival of Roman Catholicism in the late 19th century.

TURNING TO RELIGION

During the 1880s and 1890s, the world was changing rapidly and many French people turned to the Roman Catholic church for a sense of security and tradition. As a result, many donated money to build the Sacré-Coeur (the "Sacred Heart"), a dazzling white church that sits on top of a hill in Montmartre, Paris. Gauguin was not religious but he created many religious paintings and respected other people's faiths. Like other Symbolist painters, he was interested in showing the inner, spiritual world of human beings.

◀ People in Le Pouldu earned money gathering seaweed. This seaweed gatherer is holding the same tool as the man in the background of *The Green Christ*.

A DIFFICULT MAN

In July of 1890, van Gogh committed suicide by shooting himself in the chest with a pistol. Gauguin wrote a letter of sympathy to van Gogh's brother Theo, but did not go to the funeral. He also upset Émile Bernard by refusing to help him organize an exhibition of van Gogh's paintings. Many of Gauguin's friends were finding it more and more difficult to deal with his single-minded selfishness and avoided his company. Gauguin even offended his oldest and most faithful friend, Schuffenecker.

TIMELINE ▶

October 1889	July 27, 1890	November 1890	January 25, 1891
Gauguin returns to Pont-Aven then goes to live at Le Pouldu.	Vincent van Gogh tries to commit suicide by shooting himself in the chest. He dies two days later.	Gauguin leaves Le Pouldu for Paris, where he mixes with the Symbolist poets and painters.	Theo van Gogh, Gauguin's art dealer and brother of Vincent, dies of bronchitis.

The Green Christ, 1889

oil on canvas, 36 $^1/_4$ x 29 in (92 x 73.5 cm), Musée Royaux des Beaux-Arts de Belgique, Brussels, Belgium

Gauguin based the statue in the painting on a moss-covered calvary near Pont-Aven (see page 15). In the background, a seaweed gatherer returns from the beach.

Escape to the Tropics

THE NABIS

THE NABIS

In 1888, Gauguin taught student artist Paul Sérusier how to paint in his Synthetist style (see pages 18-19). Under Gauguin's guidance Sérusier painted a small picture on the lid of a cigar box (below). Back in Paris, Sérusier showed it to fellow artists, including Maurice Denis, Pierre Bonnard (1867-1947), and Edouard Vuillard (1868-1940). They began to paint following Gauguin's example, using colors and shapes in an imaginative way. These artists called themselves the Nabis, which means "prophets," and they were active until 1899.

▲ *The Talisman*, 1888, **Paul Sérusier.** This little oil painting is one of the landmarks of modern art.

Gauguin was a rising star in the art world. He was hailed as the leading Symbolist artist (see pages 26-27) and was friendly with many important writers and poets. Nevertheless, Gauguin remained very poor and still had not won wider recognition. The few people who bought his paintings were often wealthy eccentrics who valued Gauguin's work for its strangeness.

◄ Before he left for Tahiti, Gauguin went to say goodbye to his wife and children in Copenhagen. This photograph was taken during the three-week visit and shows Gauguin together with his son Emil and daughter Aline.

SETTING SAIL

Despite his growing success and influence, Gauguin was restless and unhappy. He had dreamt of returning to the Tropics and setting up a studio there for a long time. He was determined to put his plans into action but had no money. Gauguin held an auction of his paintings which raised over 7,000 francs – now he could go traveling. After visting his wife and family in Copenhagen, Gauguin set sail for the Pacific island of Tahiti on April 7, 1891.

MATAIEA

Gauguin arrived in the Tahitian capital, Papeete, but did not like it. He went on to live in the remote, beautiful village of Mataiea. There, he was happy and able to work hard. He painted pictures of Tahiti's lush, vibrant landscapes and the island's men and women. He often gave his paintings Tahitian titles, writing them on the canvas (see opposite).

TIMELINE ►

March 1891	March 7, 1891	March 23, 1891	April 7, 1891	June 9, 1891	September 1891
Critic Albert Aurier (1865-92) praises Gauguin as the leader of the Symbolist painters.	Gauguin arrives in Copenhagen to say goodbye to his family.	The Symbolists hold a banquet in Paris in Gauguin's honor.	Gauguin sets sail from Marseilles for Tahiti.	Gauguin arrives in Papeete, the capital of Tahiti.	Gauguin moves to Mataiea.

Vahine no te Tiare, 1891

oil on canvas, 27 3/4 x 18 3/10 in (70.5 x 46.5 cm), Ny Carlsberg Glyptotek, Copenhagen, Denmark

Gauguin painted *Vahine no te Tiare*, which means *Woman with a Flower*, soon after his arrival in Mataiea. Traditionally Tahitian women wore a wraparound skirt called a *pareo* and left their chest bare, but French Christian missionaries encouraged them to wear European clothes. In this painting the Tahitian woman wears her best clothes – a blue dress with a lacy collar and sleeves.

31

Tahiti

Tahiti is one of the largest islands in the South Pacific. It forms part of Polynesia, a group of far-flung islands in an area called Oceania. This area includes New Zealand, Hawaii, Easter Island, Fiji, and Tonga. The native people of Polynesia are known as Polynesians. Scholars believe that the Polynesians migrated to the islands from Southeast Asia about 4,000 years ago.

A COLONY

During the 18th and 19th centuries, France and Britain seized many of the Polynesian islands and made them part of their empires. Tahiti was put under French rule in 1842.

The Polynesian people suffered a great deal after the arrival of the Europeans. They had no resistance to European diseases such as the common cold, and tens of thousands of Polynesians died. Christian missionaries destroyed the Polynesians' temples and statues, and forbade

A hand-colored photograph of Tahitian women on a veranda in Papeete, c. 1907. Until 1836, when the first European missionaries introduced the long dresses that these women are wearing, many had only worn a skirt. This change was just a small part in the gradual destruction of the traditional Tahitian way of life through colonization.

them to wear tattoos or take part in traditional dances. Most Polynesians became Christians. They worked for the French in plantations or as servants in their homes.

TRAVELERS' TALES

European travelers to Tahiti described the island as a kind of paradise. They claimed the Tahitian people were like happy, friendly children and life on the island was always easy and peaceful. Some Europeans also argued that the Polynesians were an inferior, primitive race, therefore Europeans had a right and a duty to rule them.

FRENCH POLYNESIA

Marquesas Islands

Hiva Oa

Tuamotu Islands

Fangataufa

Society Islands

Tahiti

Mururoa

Tubuai Islands

Gambier Islands

THE 21ST CENTURY

French Polynesia is part of Oceania and remains an overseas territory of France. France has used the territory's remote atolls (sunken islands) of Mururoa and Fangataufa to test its nuclear weapons. In 1996, these tests caused violent protests in Papeete. Today many Polynesian people want their islands to be independent.

The 118 islands of French Polynesia are scattered over 1,158,301 square miles of the South Pacific Ocean.

Before going to Tahiti, Gauguin believed many of the stories he heard about the island. He thought that Europe had become a rotten and dishonest place and that Tahiti, by contrast, was an unspoiled world. In 1889, he wrote to a friend: "the Tahitians … experience only the sweet things of life. For them, living means only singing and loving."

PARADISE LOST

After arriving in Tahiti, Gauguin saw that it was very far from being a paradise. He realized that much of the Tahitians' traditional way of life had been lost. At first glance Gauguin's Tahitian paintings seem to show us a sunny, happy world, full of youth and beauty. They are painted in hot, brilliant colors: pinks and reds, oranges and yellows, and

▲ *Maori Girl in a Canoe*, 1879, Nicolas Chevalier. Before Gauguin, French painters portrayed the Polynesians in a very romantic way. This "Maori" (Polynesian) girl lazing in a canoe does not look very Polynesian at all. Gauguin, by contrast, tried to show the real appearance of Polynesian men and women.

rich blues. If we look closer, we notice that there is a great deal of sadness in these pictures.

During Gauguin's stay, he sometimes defended the rights of the Tahitians. He attacked the French government in local newspapers and encouraged the Polynesians to resist their rulers' abuses of power. Even today Gauguin remains a controversial figure in Tahiti. Many Polynesians consider him to have been like any other French colonist who exploited their homeland just as much as the plantation owners and other settlers. Others think that his paintings show a great sensitivity to Polynesian culture and attempted to unite two very different cultures.

◀ *Upaupa*, 1891. In this painting, Gauguin shows a traditional Tahitian firelit dance. Under French rule these dances were outlawed so it is not known if Gauguin actually saw this scene.

In Search of Recognition

▲ *Noa Noa* was first published in 1925, 22 years after Gauguin's death. Since 1925, *Noa Noa* has been translated into all the major European languages and hundreds of thousands of copies have been sold.

NOA NOA

While in Paris, Gauguin wrote a 38-page manuscript full of tales about Tahitian customs and legends, as well as his own experiences in Tahiti. He called the book *Noa Noa*, which means "Very Fragrant." Gauguin wrote to Mette about his project: "I am going to bring out a book … that will tell about my life in Tahiti and the way I feel about art." Gauguin worked on *Noa Noa* between 1894 and 1897. The 38 pages grew to 204 pages, illustrated with 10 woodcuts, 31 watercolors, 7 photographs, and 2 drawings.

In the spring of 1892 Gauguin became very ill – he began spitting blood and was rushed to the hospital with a suspected heart attack. In the months of recovery that followed, he decided that he must get back to Paris but he had used up all of the money raised by the sale of his paintings in 1891. After borrowing money from a friend Gauguin arrived back in Marseilles on August 23, 1893, with 66 paintings and great hopes for an exhibition that would finally establish his name.

PARIS

The famous Durand-Ruel Gallery, which showed many avant-garde artists' work, agreed to sell Gauguin's work and his hopes for recognition soared. On November 10, Gauguin exhibited 40 paintings and two sculptures. The exhibition received good reviews, stirred up a lot of interest in the press, and sold 11 paintings.

Despite his success, Gauguin found the French capital unfriendly. To many Parisians Gauguin seemed like a savage. He wore a big blue cape and white gloves and carried a carved cane. People found his bold paintings of Polynesian women "barbaric" and even frightening.

◄ The mysterious statues, or *moia*, of Easter Island (Rapa Nui) helped fire Gauguin's imagination when painting pictures of the Tahitians' religion. The *moia* are stone giants, averaging about 15 feet (4.6 m) tall.

TIMELINE ▶

Spring 1892	August 23, 1893	November 10, 1893	April 1894	July 1895
Gauguin is very ill with a suspected heart attack. Spends time in hospital.	Gauguin arrives back in Paris.	40 of Gauguin's Tahitian paintings and two sculptures are exhibited at the Durand-Ruel Gallery in Paris. 11 paintings are sold.	Gauguin goes to Pont-Aven.	Gauguin leaves France for the last time.

Arearea no Varua, 1892

oil on canvas, 29 1/2 x 37 in (75 x 94 cm), Musée d'Orsay, Paris, France

This painting is full of mystery. Its title means *The Amusement of the Evil Spirit*, so perhaps the dog is a *tupapa'u*, or an evil spirit of the dead.

In some of his paintings, Gauguin showed Polynesian legends and ceremonies. There were no temples or statues left on Tahiti, so he often used the art of other religions to help him imagine what they might have looked like. In *Arearea no Varua*, one of the women sits like an Indian Buddha. In the background, Tahitians are worshipping a huge statue like the ones found on Easter Island (see left).

"I traveled third class [from Tahiti], penned in with a troop of two hundred soldiers. In order to be able to move each man was allotted fifty square centimeters [eight square inches] on the foredeck in between the sheep... And that's how it was for forty days... If it weren't for the sea one would much rather walk."

Paul Gauguin

Depression and Despair

▲ *In the Time of Harmony, 1894-95,*
Paul Signac (see page 12). Signac
shows a seaside paradise where people
work and play together happily,
whereas the figures in Gauguin's
seaside paradise (opposite) look sad.

GAUGUIN'S FAMILIES

Gauguin lived with a series of
native women, or *vahines,* in
Polynesia. The vahines kept
house for him, posed for him,
and bore him children. Gauguin
kept these relationships secret in
his letters to Mette. The final
break between Mette and
Gauguin came in 1894 when
Mette discovered, not the secret
of his other families, but that
Gauguin had inherited a lot of
money and refused to give any
of it to her and the children.
After enduring years of hardship
for Gauguin, Mette finally gave
up her hopes of a life with him.

Gauguin was depressed at his lack of long-term
success in the Parisian art world and was
anxious to return to Polynesia. In September of
1895, he arrived back in Tahiti and went to live in a
small, isolated village called Punaauia. There
Gauguin lived in a large thatched house, took a
Tahitian wife named Pahura, and wore traditional
Tahitian dress. By this time Gauguin's health had
become very bad – he had a sore on his foot that
refused to get better and suffered constantly from
fevers – so he could only paint from time to time.

A SUICIDE ATTEMPT

In 1897 Gauguin's daughter, Aline, died of pneumonia. She
was only 20 years old. Heartbroken, Gauguin painted *Where
Do We Come From? What Are We? Where Are We Going?*
(opposite) – the largest picture he had ever attempted. In
this painting, he tried to express all the sadness he felt about
life.

After finishing the picture Gauguin went to some nearby
woods and swallowed arsenic (a poison) in an attempt to kill
himself. However, he threw up most of the arsenic and spent
two days in agony. Finally, he crawled back down to his hut,
depressed and exhausted.

▶ **Gauguin's
house in Punaauia
was large and
comfortable. He
even had a special
studio built to
paint in.**

TIMELINE ▶

September 1895	April 1897	April 1897
Gauguin arrives back in Tahiti.	Aline Gauguin dies of pneumonia.	Gauguin paints *Where Do We Come From? What Are We? Where Are We Going?* in just a few days and then attempts suicide.

Where Do We Come From? What Are We?
Where Are We Going?, 1897

oil on canvas, 54 ³/4 x 147 ¹/2 in (139.1 x 374.6 cm), Museum of Fine Arts Boston (Tompkins Collection),
Boston, Massachusetts

Where Do We Come From? What Are We? Where Are We Going? asks big questions about life. On the right of
the painting, an innocent baby lies on the floor; on the left, a dying old woman hides her face in her hands; in the
middle, a man reaches up to pluck a fruit. Both Gauguin and Signac (see *In the Time of Harmony*, opposite)
include a man plucking fruit in their paintings to symbolize the pursuit of knowledge, which is a reference to the
Bible where Adam and Eve pluck an apple from the Tree of Knowledge. While Signac believed that knowledge
gives people dignity, Gauguin believed that knowledge led to sin and misery.

*"Before dying I put all my energy into it [Where Do We Come
From? What Are We? Where Are We Going?], such a painful
passion under terrible circumstances, and a vision so clear
without corrections that the haste [in which I made the
painting] disappears and the life surges up."*

Paul Gauguin

37

Final Days

In 1898, again desperate for money, Gauguin took a job as an illustrator in the French colonial government's Department of Housing. Here he argued with his employers, increasingly turned to alcohol, and painted very little.

HIVA OA

In 1901, exhausted, ill, and tired of fighting with the authorities, Gauguin left Tahiti for Hiva Oa, one of the remote Marquesas Islands in the far north of French Polynesia (621 miles east of Tahiti). Gauguin's wild and unspoiled new home gave him fresh hope and energy. He painted colorful, light-filled landscapes and horseback riders galloping on the beach. He also took a new wife, or vahine.

THE OUTCAST

Most of the French settlers on Hiva Oa avoided Gauguin because of his drinking, his wild parties, and his hatred of the authorities. While all of this hostility was growing, Gauguin's health was quickly deteriorating. His legs were so badly swollen with sores that he could hardly walk, he was losing his sight, and he was drinking too much. On May 8, 1903, his body finally destroyed by alcohol and years of illness, Gauguin had a heart attack and died in his hut.

▲ A Roman-Egyptian grave painting of the 2nd or 3rd century A.D.

◄ Gauguin's grave is in the Catholic graveyard on the island of Hiva Oa. It is decorated with one of his small sculptures.

ANCIENT PORTRAITS

The style of Gauguin's self-portrait opposite was inspired by a copy of a portrait he had, like the one above, of a Roman who lived in Egypt around 300 A.D. Such portraits were painted on the coffin cases that held a person's mummified remains to remind people what their dead relative looked like. Perhaps Gauguin was aware that, like the man in the picture, he would soon be dead.

TIMELINE ▶

1898	1900	September 1901	September 14, 1902	May 8, 1903
Gauguin's Tahitian wife, Pahura, gives birth to their son Emile.	Clovis Gauguin, the son Gauguin had taken to live with him in Paris for two years (1885-87), tragically dies of blood poisoning after routine surgery.	Gauguin arrives in Hiva Oa.	Gauguin's Marquesan wife, Vaeoho, gives birth to their daughter Tahiatikaomata.	Gauguin dies of a heart attack, alone in his hut.

Self-Portrait, 1903

oil on canvas, 16 1/2 x 9 2/5 in
(42 x 24 cm), Kunstmuseum, Basel,
Germany

In the last year of his life, Gauguin
painted this sad and simple self-
portrait. His earlier self-portraits are
full of confidence and defiance. In
this painting, he looks out at us very
calmly and truthfully. Even the
painting's colors are cooler, as if to
match Gauguin's quieter mood.
Gauguin's face almost fills the
picture space – making him seem
even more alone.

*"No later than last night I dreamed I was dead and, oddly
enough, it was the true instant when I was living happily."*

Paul Gauguin

Gauguin's Legacy

Gauguin was a legend in his own lifetime. After he left for Tahiti, people back in Paris gossiped about how he had given up everything – his wife, children, job, and finally his homeland – for the sake of his art. After his death, Gauguin's reputation as a great painter grew. People everywhere came to think of him as a heroic and romantic figure, whose often unhappy life showed the great sacrifice that every genius has to make. While there was some truth in such stories, there was a great deal of myth, too. Gauguin's own notebooks and diaries – which often didn't tell the truth – encouraged this popular view of his life.

▲ *In the Rain*, 1912, Franz Marc. Marc's use of color to express emotions was taken from Gauguin's work. Marc was one of the founding members of the German Blaue Reiter (Blue Rider) Expressionist art movement (1911-14).

▲ The artist Georges Braque in his studio, 1910. Like Gauguin, Braque used bright colors, especially in his work as a Fauve artist.

AN INSPIRATION

Gauguin's life and work inspired many other painters. In 1906, the first big exhibition of Gauguin's paintings was held in Paris. Artists such as Henri Matisse (1869-1954) and Georges Braque (1882-1963) admired Gauguin's work deeply. At this time, these artists were already creating paintings so full of violent colors that a critic called them the Fauves, or the "Wild Beasts." Gauguin's example gave them the courage to take their experiments even further and taught them that what was important in art was the imagination and creativity of the artist.

In Germany a group of artists known as the Expressionists – including Ernst Kirchner (1880-1938), Franz Marc (1880-1916), and Emil Nolde (1867-1956) – saw Gauguin as a pioneer of their art, with its strange, brilliant colors and evocation of a wild and "primitive" way of life. Artists everywhere followed Gauguin's example and left big cities to work in remote and unspoiled places.

A HERO?

After the horror and destruction of World War I (1914-18), many people thought that European civilization had shown how deeply corrupt it was. Gauguin's escape from Paris and from his conventional, middle-class life began to seem idealistic rather than selfish. In 1919 the English writer Somerset Maugham (1874-1965) wrote a best-selling novel, *The Moon and Sixpence*, that took its inspiration from Gauguin's life. In the novel an English artist named Strickland deserts his wife to live as a painter on a tropical island. Maugham depicts Strickland as a highly romantic figure and the book even inspired a Hollywood film.

▲ A scene from the Hollywood film *The Moon and Sixpence*, 1942, based on Gauguin's life on the island of Tahiti.

A COMPLICATED LEGACY

We have recently learned a great deal about Gauguin's life. The letters written between Gauguin and his wife, Mette, reveal a complicated and sad relationship. Some critics have also reassessed Gauguin's life in Tahiti, suggesting that he exploited the island and its people for his own purposes without any real understanding of their way of life. When France used Polynesian atolls as nuclear-testing sites in 1996, some Polynesians pointed out the gap between the paradise-like image the French imposed on the island (as seen in Gauguin's paintings) and the environmental harm they were ready to inflict.

A PAINTER OF DREAMS

For all of the controversy that still surrounds him, Gauguin's paintings continue to inspire. His images – whether of rural Brittany or tropical Tahiti – still act as powerful magnets for dreams of a different and simpler way of life.

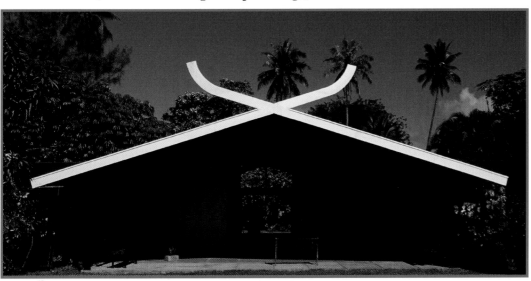

◀ The Gauguin Museum in Papeari, Tahiti, is a modern building based on traditional Tahitian architecture. The museum contains photos of Gauguin and of Tahiti during Gauguin's stay there, as well as some of his sculptures and watercolors.

Friends and Foes

The story of the relationship between Paul Gauguin and Vincent van Gogh is one of the most famous in the history of art. Both artists were passionate about their work – and sensitive to criticisms of it. Their stay together in Arles, in 1888, was destined to be difficult.

▲ *Paul Gauguin's Armchair*, **1888, Vincent van Gogh.** Van Gogh painted this picture during Gauguin's stay with him. The chair is sturdy and comfortable. Van Gogh also painted his own seat, that of a poor and humble peasant.

BROTHER ARTISTS

Van Gogh looked forward to Gauguin's arrival in Arles. Van Gogh believed that artists should be like brothers, exchanging pictures and sharing ideas – he wanted to set up a "Studio of the South."

"I must tell you that even while I am working I think continually about the plan of setting up a studio in which you and I will be permanent residents, but which both of us want to turn into a shelter and refuge for friends, against the time when they find that the struggle is getting too much for them."

▲ **Van Gogh writing to Gauguin about his plans for a "Studio of the South," October 3, 1888.**

THE STUDIO OF THE SOUTH

Van Gogh's "Studio of the South" lasted just nine weeks. Each artist painted in a very different way (see page 22), and Gauguin's personality was much more powerful than van Gogh's. Gauguin acted as if he were the teacher and van Gogh the pupil.

TIMELINE ▶

1848	1871	1884	1886	1888
June 7, 1848 Paul Gauguin is born in Paris, France.	**April 1871** Gauguin returns to Paris and becomes a stockbroker.	**July 1884** Mette takes the children to Copenhagen.	**October 1886** Gauguin returns to Paris.	**February 1888** Gauguin leaves Paris for Pont-Aven.
October 1851 Gauguin's family leaves France for Peru; his father dies on the way.	**November 22, 1873** Gauguin marries Mette Gad.	**November 1884** Gauguin joins his family in Copenhagen.	**Winter 1886-87** Gauguin works on *Four Breton Women* in Paris.	**Summer 1888** Gauguin meets Émile Bernard.
1855 Gauguin's family returns to France.	**1883** Gauguin loses his job and becomes a full-time painter.	**June 1885** Gauguin returns to Paris. He takes his son Clovis with him.	**April 10, 1887** Gauguin sails for Panama with the painter Charles Laval.	**August-September 1888** Gauguin paints *The Vision After the Sermon*.
1865 Gauguin joins the merchant navy.	**January 1884** Gauguin takes his family to live in Rouen.	**July 1886** Gauguin goes to paint in Pont-Aven, Brittany.	**June 1887** Gauguin and Laval travel to Martinique.	**October 23, 1888** Gauguin joins Vincent van Gogh at the Yellow House in Arles, southern France.
			November 1887 Gauguin returns to Paris.	

◀ **August 1888, Gauguin in a letter to Schuffenecker. It is not hard to imagine that he tried to convince van Gogh of the same thing during their stay together.**

▶ **Early in 1889, van Gogh wrote to Émile Bernard about how Gauguin had almost tempted him into "abstraction." Van Gogh means that Gauguin persuaded him to paint using his imagination rather than allowing him to paint exactly what was in front of him, as was his habit.**

"When Gauguin was in Arles, as you know I once or twice allowed myself to be led into abstractions. At the time, this road seemed to me a charming track. But it's an enchanted land, my dear friend, and soon one finds oneself up against an unclimbable wall."

Van Gogh felt threatened by Gauguin, and Gauguin grew tired of their stressful life together. Finally, on December 23, van Gogh and Gauguin had a violent argument and Gauguin left. In the aftermath of the argument van Gogh cut off part of his left ear in a cry for help.

A TURNING POINT

For both artists, the "Studio of the South" was a turning-point in their careers. Gauguin felt even more sure that he needed to get away from France and live and work alone. Perhaps he also felt partly responsible for van Gogh's breakdown, and believed that he could not be a good friend to anyone.

For van Gogh, Gauguin's stay in Arles was disastrous. He never really recovered his sanity. After two spells in mental asylums, he finally entered the care of a doctor in the town of Auvers-sur-Oise. All the while, he painted furiously, producing some of his greatest masterpieces. In July of 1890, he shot himself and died two days later. Gauguin did not go to his friend's funeral.

"Alas I see myself condemned to be less and less understood, and I must resign myself to following my path alone ... The savage will return to the wilderness."

▲ **Gauguin in his last letter to van Gogh, June 1890.**

1888	1889	1891	1893	1895
December 23, 1888 Van Gogh and Gauguin have a terrible argument; Gauguin leaves the Yellow House for Paris; van Gogh cuts off part of his left ear.	**October 1889** Gauguin goes to live at Le Pouldu.	**March 7, 1891** Gauguin goes to Copenhagen to say goodbye to his family.	**August 23, 1893** Gauguin arrives back in Paris.	**September 1895** Gauguin arrives back in Tahiti.
February 1889 Gauguin returns to Brittany from Paris.	**July 29, 1890** Van Gogh dies of a self-inflicted gun shot. Gauguin does not go to the funeral.	**April 7, 1891** Gauguin sets sail from Marseilles for the island of Tahiti.	**November 10, 1893** Gauguin exhibits 40 of his paintings and two sculptures at the Durand-Ruel Gallery in Paris.	**April 1897** Aline Gauguin dies suddenly of pneumonia.
Summer 1889 Gauguin and his friends hold an exhibition of their work at the Café Volpini.	**November 1890** Gauguin leaves Le Pouldu for Paris, where he mixes with the Symbolist poets.	**June 9, 1891** Gauguin arrives in Papeete, the capital of Tahiti, then moves on to Mataiea.	**April 1894** Gauguin goes to Pont-Aven.	**1900** Clovis Gauguin dies after surgery.
	February 23, 1891 Gauguin holds an auction of his work to raise money.	**Spring 1892** Gauguin has a heart attack, spends time in the hospital.	**July 1895** Gauguin leaves France for the last time.	**September 1901** Gauguin goes to Hiva Oa.
				May 8, 1903 Gauguin dies in his hut on Hiva Oa.

Glossary

abstraction: in art, a style of painting or drawing that creates pictures that are independent of reality; such pictures may sometimes be based on a landscape, person, or some other object seen in the real world, but are made up of colors and lines used for their own sake.

art critic: a person who makes a living out of writing about art.

art dealer: a person who buys and sells art to make a living.

avant-garde: describes new, experimental, or radical ideas. From the French for vanguard, the first troops into battle.

Buddha: a Northern Indian nobleman of the 6th-5th centuries B.C. who attained Enlightenment – a perfect state of being – having rejected greed, money, and hatred. In art, a painting or sculpture of Buddha or a follower of Buddha who has attained Enlightenment.

corrupt: something that is dishonest, or decaying. In a person, moral collapse.

empire: a large number of countries ruled by a more powerful country.

exhibition: a public showing of art works.

Expressionism: an approach to painting which communicates an emotional state of mind rather than external reality.

immunity: resistance to disease.

Impressionism: an art movement created by a group of artists based in Paris during the late-19th century who painted "impressions" of the world with broad brushstrokes of pure color. The group included Pierre-Auguste Renoir (1841-1919), Claude Monet (1840-1926), Camille Pissarro (1830-1903), and Edgar Degas (1834-1917).

landscape: in painting, a picture of the countryside.

malaria: a tropical disease passed on to humans by the bite of an infected mosquito. Malaria causes hot and cold fevers and can lead to death.

missionary: someone who tries to convert others to a religion different than the one they were born into. Christian missionaries traveled all over the world during the 19th century preaching the teachings of Jesus Christ.

palette: a flat board on which artists arrange their oil paints that are ready for use.

pareo: a wraparound skirt traditionally worn in Tahiti by both men and women.

peninsula: a thin strip of land that juts into the sea from the mainland.

plantation: a large area of land reserved for the cultivation of tropical crops, such as rubber, coffee, or bananas.

pneumonia: an illness where the lungs become filled with water, making a person unable to breath.

portrait: an image of a person, usually of their face, which tries to capture their personality.

Prussia: a former state in north and central modern-day Germany, once a military power. Prussia was dissolved in 1947 and divided between East and West Germany.

Realism: a style of art that developed in mid-19th century France. The Realists painted ordinary, everyday subjects as truthfully as possible. The most important Realist artist was Gustave Courbet (1819-77).

republic: a country where governing power is held by a person or persons elected by the people, not by a monarch.

Roman Catholicism: one of the major Christian churches; the leader of the Roman Catholic Church is the Pope, who lives in Vatican City, Rome.

still life: a picture of objects that do not move, usually carefully arranged by the artist.

stockbroker: someone who buys and sells stocks (shares in companies) for profit.

stock exchange: a place where stocks are traded by stockbrokers.

Tropics: the parts of the Earth in between the Tropics of Cancer and Capricorn, and on either side of the Equator. The Tropics are hot and humid. Polynesia and Peru are both tropical countries.

Museums and Galleries

Works by Gauguin are exhibited in museums and galleries all around the world. Even if you can't visit any of these galleries yourself, you may be able to visit their web sites. Gallery web sites often show pictures of the artworks they have on display. Some of the web sites even offer virtual tours which allow you to wander around and look at different paintings while sitting comfortably in front of your computer!

Most of the international web sites detailed below include an option that allows you to view them in English.

EUROPE

Copenhagen Ny Carlsberg Glyptotek
Dantes Plads 7
DK-1566
København V, Denmark
www.glyptoteket.dk/index-uk.html

Courtauld Institute of Art
Somerset House
Strand
London WC2R ORN
England, UK
www.courtauld.ac.uk

Musée d'Orsay
Quai Anatole France
Paris 7e
France
www.musee-orsay.fr

National Gallery of Scotland
The Mound
Edinburgh EH2
Scotland, UK
www.nationalgalleries.org

State Hermitage Museum
Embankment of River Neva
St. Petersburg
Russia
www.hermitagemuseum.org

Tate Modern
Bankside
London SE1 9TG
England, UK
www.tate.org.uk

UNITED STATES

Albright-Knox Art Gallery
1285 Elwood Avenue
Buffalo, NY 14222-1096
www.albrightknox.org

Art Institute of Chicago
111 South Michigan Avenue
Chicago, IL 60603
www.artic.edu

Baltimore Museum of Art
10 Art Museum Drive
Baltimore, MD 21218-3898
www.artbma.org

Metropolitan Museum of Art
1000 Fifth Avenue (at 82nd Street)
New York, NY 10028-0198
www.metmuseum.org

Museum of Fine Arts
465 Huntington Avenue
Boston, MA 02115-5523
www.boston.com/mfa/

National Gallery of Art
6th Street & Constitution Avenue N.W.
Washington, D.C. 20565
www.nga.gov

OCEANIA

Gauguin Museum
PK51 200 Papeari
BP 16019-98727
Tahiti

Index

Arearea no Varua 35

Be Mysterious 24
Bernard, Émile 18, 21, 24, 28, 43
Braque, Georges 40
Breton Women at a Pardon
    (Bouvert) 15
Brittany 6, 12, 13, 14, 15, 16, 24,
    41, 42, 43

Café Volpini 24, 43
Copenhagen 10, 20, 30, 42, 43

Denis, Maurice 18, 30
Durand-Ruel Gallery 34, 43

Easter Island 34, 35
Expressionists 40, 44

Four Breton Women 12, 13, 14,
    15, 42
France, South of 20
    religious revival in 28
    the Republic 6, 8
    the Second Empire 6, 8
Franco-Prussian War 8

The Garden in the Rue Carcel 9
Gauguin, Paul
    and Japanese art 25
    as a stockbroker 8, 9, 42
    early life 6-7, 8
    ill-health 16, 34, 36, 38, 43
    in Arles 22, 42, 43
    in Hiva Oa 38, 43
    in Le Pouldu 28, 43
    in Martinique 16, 17, 18, 42
    in Panama 16
    in Paris 6, 8, 9, 10, 12, 14, 16,
        18, 20, 24, 34, 42, 43
    in Pont-Aven 14, 15, 16, 18,
        24, 28, 34, 42, 43
    in Punaauia 36
    in Rouen 10, 42
    in South of France 20
    in Tahiti 30-34, 35, 36
    pottery 24
    sculpture 24, 34, 38, 41

suicide attempt 36
Symbolist work 19, 27, 28, 29,
    37
Synthetism 18-19, 30
vahines 36, 38
wood carvings 24
Gauguin, Aline (mother) 6, 7, 8
    Aline (daughter) 8, 30, 36, 37,
        43
    Clovis (father) 6, 7, 42
    Clovis (son) 8, 10, 12, 16, 38,
        42, 43
    Marie (sister) 7, 12, 16
    Mette (wife) 8, 9, 10, 16, 34,
        36, 41, 42
    other Gauguin children 8, 38
Gauguin Museum, Papeari 41, 45
van Gogh, Theo 20, 22, 28
    Vincent, 20-21, 22, 23, 28,
        42-43
The Green Christ 28, 29

de Hann, Jacob Meyer 18, 28
Hugo, Victor 20, 21

Impressionists 9, 12, 13, 19, 20,
    22, 26, 27, 44
In the Rain (Marc) 40
In the Time of Harmony (Signac)
    36, 37

The Laughing Spider (Redon) 27
Laval, Charles 16, 24, 42

Mallarmé, Stéphane 26, 27
Maori Girl in a Canoe (Chevalier)
    33
Marc, Franz 40
Maugham, Somerset 41
Monet, Claude 9, 44

the Nabis 30
Napoleon III 6, 7
Noa Noa 34

Paul Gauguin at the Age of Two
    (Laure) 6
Paul Gauguin's Armchair (van
    Gogh) 42

Peasant Pushing a Wheelbarrow
    (Pissarro) 9
Peru 6, 7, 8, 16, 17, 42, 44
Pissarro, Camille 9, 44
Pointillism 12
Polynesia 24, 32, 34, 35, 36, 38,
    41, 44
Portrait of Vincent van Gogh
    Painting Sunflowers 23
Puvis de Chavannes, Pierre 27

The Realists 26, 44
Redon, Odilon 27

Schuffenecker, Emile 9, 16, 18,
    22, 24, 28, 43
The Schuffenecker Family 25
Self-Portrait (1885) 10, 11
Self-Portrait (1903) 38, 39
Self-Portrait: Les Misérables 20, 21
Sérusier, Paul 28, 30
Seurat, Georges 12
Signac, Paul 12, 36, 37
Sunday Afternoon on the Island of
    La Grande Jatte (Seurat) 12
Symbolism 24, 26-27, 28, 30, 43
Synthetism 18, 30

Tahiti 6, 30, 32-33, 34, 35, 36,
    40, 41, 43
The Talisman (Sérusier) 30
Tristan, Flora 6
Tristan Moscosco, Don Pio de 7
Tropical Vegetation 16, 17

The Universal Exhibition 24, 25
Upaupa 33

Vahine no te Tiare 21, 31
Vase With Twelve Sunflowers (van
    Gogh) 22
The Vision After the Sermon 18, 19,
    42

Where Do We Come From? What
    Are We? Where Are We Going?
    36, 37

Winter (Chavannes) 27